Dance Arounc

Contents

Why We Dance

What do you do when you feel happy? Perhaps you laugh out loud or jump up and down. Or maybe you turn on the music and start to dance. You stomp and run and twirl. Did you know that it is not just you but people all over the world who dance when they're feeling happy?

The 1920s were a happy time in America. Young people celebrated with jazz dances such as the Charleston.

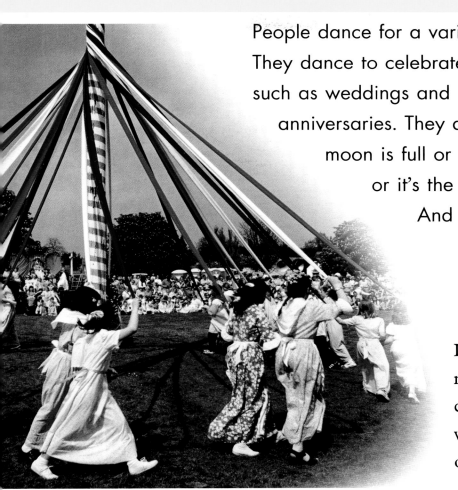

People dance for a variety of reasons. They dance to celebrate special occasions, such as weddings and birthdays and anniversaries. They dance when the moon is full or the sun is shining or it's the first day of May. And sometimes they dance just for the fun of it.

In many countries, maypole dances celebrate the end of winter and the return of flowers.

3

People dance all around the world, but not all dances are the same, because people from diverse cultures have unique histories and, therefore, different reasons for dancing. Certain African dances tell the heartbreaking saga of slaves who were stolen from their families. Some lively Inuit dances celebrate the harpooning of whales, which are then shared by the people in the village.

A member of the Nambe Pueblo performs the Buffalo Dance in New Mexico, USA.

Dance Around the World

Written by
Dina Anastasio

Photograph credits: © **Alison Wright/Corbis:** p. 7 Maculelê; © **Altrendo Images/Getty Images:** p. 18; © **Ariel Skelley/Corbis:** p. 23 flower ballerinas; © **Bob Krist/Corbis:** title page; © **Craig Aurness/Corbis:** p. 4; © **Craig Lovell/Corbis:** pp. 14–15; © **Earl & Nazima Kowall:** p. 9 tinikling; © **Ed Kashi/ Corbis:** p. 11; © **Edimédia/Corbis:** p. 5; © **Gail Mooney/Corbis:** p. 10; **Getty Images:** p. 12; © **Gideon Mendel/Corbis:** p. 3; © **Hulton Archive/Getty Images:** p. 2; © **Jeremy Horner/Corbis:** pp. 23 dancers with headdresses; © **John Springer Collection/Corbis:** p. 20; © **Kevin Burke/Corbis:** cover (Ukrainian dancers); © **Larry Williams/Corbis:** p. 22 girl with raised arm; © **Lawrence Migdale/Getty Images:** p. 19; © **Martin Bureau/AFP/Getty Images:** p. 13; © **Matthew McKee; Eye Ubiquitous/Corbis:** p. 22 Aborigine boy; © **Michael S. Yamashita/Corbis:** p. 22 Hawaiian girl; © **Michel Setboun/Corbis:** p. 9 capoeira; © **Morton Beebe/Corbis:** p. 8; © **Pablo Corral V/Corbis:** p. 9 flamenco; © **Paul W. Liebhardt/Corbis:** p. 22 African girls; © **Richard A. Cooke/Corbis:** p. 6 hula dancers; © **Setboun/Corbis:** p. 7 Korean fan dance; © **Stephanie Maze/Corbis:** cover (Korean dancers— background); © **Stephen Stickler/Getty Images:** p. 21; © **Swift/Vanuga Images/Corbis:** pp. 22–23 Native American girls; © **Ted Streshinsky/Corbis:** pp. 16–17; © **Tim Graham/ Corbis Sygma:** p. 6 Maori dancers, p. 9 manjiani; © **Tony Hopewell/Getty Images:** p. 9 polka; © **Wally McNamee/Corbis:** p. 7 Chinese ribbon dance

www.WrightGroup.com

Wright Group

Copyright © 2006 by Wright Group/McGraw-Hill.

Printed in the United States of America.

Send all inquiries to:
Wright Group/McGraw-Hill
P.O. Box 812960
Chicago, IL 60681

ISBN 1-4045-3757-0
ISBN 1-4045-4065-2 (6-pack)

1 2 3 4 5 6 7 8 9 PBM 11 10 09 08 07 06 05

The McGraw·Hill Companies

Many dances portray the personal history of the performers, while others describe actual historical events. Still other dances recount fictional stories that have been handed down for generations.

Some dances began as a way to entertain kings. The first ballet dances, or court ballets, occurred in Italy, where performers danced stories for the king's amusement. The important element of these early ballets was not the stories they portrayed, but rather the visual display created by the fancy costumes and the scenery.

The first ballets were danced in Italy centuries ago.

5

How We Dance

Dancers use their feet, hands, and sometimes their whole bodies to tell their stories. Hula dancers in Hawaii tell stories with their hands. Angry hands tell stories of fierce battles, and flowing hands tell softer stories about peace

In Hawaii, hula dancers tell the stories of their ancestors.

and love. Maori dancers use their faces to express defiance and ridicule. They stick out their tongues, pop their eyes, and slap their hands against their chests to frighten their enemies.

In New Zealand, Maori men dance the *haka*.

Many dancers wear detailed costumes and masks, which help enhance the story being told. They also use props such as the beautiful fans used in the Korean fan dance, the sticks that look like sugarcane used in the Brazilian *Maculelê*, and the colorful silk ribbons used in the Chinese ribbon dance.

Korean fan dance

Maculelê was created by African slaves on sugarcane plantations in Brazil.

Chinese ribbon dance

7

All Kinds of Dances

A folk dance is a traditional dance that had its beginnings among the common people, or the folk, of a nation or region. Folk dances have been passed down from generation to generation and are instrumental in helping even the youngest dancers understand their cultural heritage.

In Mexico, children learn the Mexican hat dance at an early age.

Dances from Around the World

Name of Dance	Country of Origin	Defining Features
capoeira	Brazil	combination of dance, martial arts, and acrobatics
flamenco	Spain	staccato handclapping and stamping of feet; accompanied by guitar
polka	Czechoslovakia	very fast-paced couple dance; basic pattern of hop-step-close-step
tinikling	Philippines	two people bang bamboo poles together while a dancer jumps between them
manjiani	Senegal/ West Africa	rite of passage for boys and girls; danced to the beat of a drum

capoeira   flamenco   polka   tinikling   manjiani

Many folk dances require a variety of movements, including hopping, skipping, twirling, and running. Some dances require that a dancer perform alone, while other dances are performed by groups of people who hold hands and dance in circles. There are just as many varieties of folk dances as there are varieties of people in the world!

In many Greek folk dances, dancers move in circles. The dances can be traced back to ancient Greece, over 5,000 years ago.

Young and old alike get together to dance at a *céili*, which is a social gathering in large towns and country districts of Ireland. In Ireland, people have been dancing the same happy jigs and step dances for hundreds of years.

In many places, dancing is an eagerly-anticipated activity at the end of the day. It's not just for holidays and celebrations! After laboring at their jobs all day long, people gather in streets or fields or gymnasiums to dance the night away.

11

Dancers in Bali and Thailand act out beautiful plays that have been performed for centuries. A number of these plays are religious, while others provide accounts of war, animals, kings, and comics.

The *Barong* dance from Bali tells the story of the Barong, a force of good who fights against evil.

Dancers often use their feet to communicate messages. In South Africa, miners were forbidden to talk in the mines. Frustrated and angry, they learned to talk with their feet, stamping out words with their boots. This means of communication became known as the "boot dance".

Miners in South Africa make music and words with their feet.

In America

Native Americans have been dancing since long before the first Europeans settled in America. Each tribe has its own particular dances, but certain dances are shared by Native Americans all around the Americas. Powwows, often held during the summer, are exciting celebrations of Native American traditions and spirituality. They provide an opportunity for tribes and families to get together to sing, to dance, and to renew old friendships. You can learn a great deal about Native American religion, history, and way of life by studying their dances.

The Native American hoop dance celebrates the circle of life.

Native Americans were dependent on nature for their survival. They grew their own crops, and they hunted animals that supplied them with food as well as materials for clothing and shelter. It is no surprise that many of their dances reflect both their respect for nature and their feeling of interconnectedness with it. Special dances, such as the wolf dance, honor animals. Other dances, such as the corn dance, show appreciation for the bounty of the land. Rain and sun dances ask for weather to help crops grow.

15

Early settlers in America brought with them dances from different countries and shared them with their neighbors. In time, these dances were combined to become the square dances that are still enjoyed in America today.

The pioneers helped each other build new houses, and when construction was complete, they would dance together to celebrate. For these hard-working people, square dancing was the best part of the day.

A square-dancing festival in California

17

Today, as in the past, immigrants to America bring their dances with them. Each dance is a way to share cultural backgrounds and histories, and many think that a dance is a gift of understanding. As people move from region to region and country to country, they are influenced by their new surroundings. They add new emotions, rhythms, and ways of looking at the world to their dancing.

18

The tango is a mix of African, European, and native rhythms and movements. It began in Argentina in the late 19th century.

African music and dance were carried across the ocean to America.

Some of the more modern dances, such as tap dancing, originated in America. Like boot dancing, tap dancing was a way of communicating with the feet. At first, the steps were simple and were danced on street corners, but it wasn't long before tap dancing became competitive. Each dancer tried to outdance the previous dancer. "I can do better than you," they tapped over and over. The steps grew more sophisticated and complex, and the dancers' feet flew faster and faster. In the end, the best dancers made names for themselves in their neighborhoods and across America.

Bill "Bojangles" Robinson and Shirley Temple in *The Little Colonel*

Breakdancer performing on the street in Los Angeles

In the 1970s another competitive urban dance form came along. "Breakdancing," which originated on the streets of New York, combined robotic moves, pantomime, and footwork that mirrored some martial arts. Groups of breakdancers, or B-boys, as they are called, would compete to see who had better style, more complex move combinations, or tougher moves. These so-called battles would take place on street corners and in nightclubs, accompanied by hip-hop music. Since then, breakdancing has become popular around the world, with a major international competition taking place every year in Germany.

Dance and Identity

Have you ever thought about what makes you *you?* Do you know where your ancestors were born? Do you still sing the songs that your grandparents sang when they were children? Do you still enjoy eating the same special delicacies that your ancestors brought with them to their new country?

Many people are proud of their heritage and want to be able to incorporate traditions into their daily lives. Dance is one way to keep the history of a place and of a people alive. Dances help us remember our ancestors, where they came from, and how they lived. Dance is a way to help us understand who we are.

Index

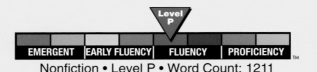

Level
P

| EMERGENT | EARLY FLUENCY | FLUENCY | PROFICIENCY |

Nonfiction • Level P • Word Count: 1211

Do you know what the Mexican hat dance and a *céili* are? Read this book to find out.

The McGraw·Hill Companies

ISBN 1-4045-3757-0

90000

9 781404 537576

Wright Group